MAHOGANY

MAHOGANY

Reflections of a Young Black Man

Josué Casa

First paperback edition November 2021
Cover design by Sheridan Davenport
Illustrations by Sheridan Davenport

ISBN: 978-1-7374653-0-0
E-ISBN: 978-1-7374653-1-7

Contributors: Scott James

Printed in the United States of America

"But by the grace of God I am what I am: and his grace which was bestowed upon me was not in vain; but I laboured more abundantly than they all: yet not I, but the grace of God which was with me."

1 Corinthians 15:10

Michael D. Hughes
Michael Akin
Terri Broussard Williams
Scott James
Christine Merdes
Maddie Barner
Chelsea Wyche
Will Manneh-Roberts
Alex Orians

Dedicated to God, My Mother, and PKB
The 3 individuals that continue to teach me that compassion is at
the core of everything we do.

TABLE OF CONTENTS

PREFACE

While everything is silent
Yet all is loud
I hear the rage
The rage that lives within this cage:

INTRODUCTION

ALL THAT I AM

Imagine, a young Black man learning to love himself. Not like
society taught me.

My skin, my ashy knees
All part of natural me.

Grateful for my heart & my mind
Cuz left up to ya'll it'd decay over time.

Realizing the world can be toxic
Especially when your skin look like chocolate.

I'm on a pedestal with a sports uniform come Sunday
Then silenced for my justice come Monday.

To you, there's no correlation
All I ever wanted was to be one in this nation.

They said fit in & fake it
I always contemplate it.

Do I do what I'm told?
Or, cop a block from Benning Road.

Prayin' to whom everything comes from
In dire need of all my dreams to come home.

Graspin' for the one to wipe my tears
Graspin' for the one to hold my fears.

Wonderin' how she sees so much promise
But can't see herself as my miss.

Learning to love me thoroughly
I is all I need inevitably.

Loving her as else
That'll always be the remission to my health.

Believe it or not
This much is true
I must love me first
In all that I do.

COMPASSION FOR ME

KNOW ME TOO

It's not on me
It's in me

Holdin' a nine
Never thought I'd see this time

Pull the trigger let it sing
Sad voices will it bring?

Repass for me
Make sure there's mac n cheese

Never seemed to fit
Maybe it's time to make life quit

Me & George Bailey relate
I see my choices & my fate

My past
They always seem to ask

As if we all don't make mistakes
Am I supposed to fake?

It's not on me
It's in me

It's just a suit
When times get hard
They'll give me the boot

This I know & this they choose
For gambling with life is what they peruse

`

Bigger & better as they would say
But I'm not just in it for the payday

To give all you've got
And still miss the knot

It's not admired to die
When all you had to do was try.

EPIPHANY

Almost took my air with a snare
Telling Him He must've made a mistake
Cuz this life ain't fair

Young black boy
How I got the world scared
Life's ambitions must be a toy

The walks through the valley
I can handle the hills
But the shallows I see more clearly

Don't say you know me
When I die
Don't hashtag me

Pursuing my goal through it all
Life moves fast
I see no fall

Losing friends again and again
They don't get it
As I arrive at my dead ends

Unrelatable to the masses I've seemed to learn
Learn to love
Do your best not to burn

As I hear my heartbeat
I wonder
Can life get any more deep?

Life moves slow
For those who came
For those who did everything and grow

We are two different people
Don't step in my circle
Trying to look through the peep hole

With all my love I extend
It grows
Hard to write my feelings to the end

Awakening at the place I started
Accepting my truths
I've stopped darted

Here I am without fuss
We're here together
Together is a must.

THE LIFE I LIVE

I was runnin' the course
But now I'm takin' the lead
No matter what I do
I feel like Life's steed

Pushin' through the pain
Winnin' no matter what their name
Wonder when the bell rings
Will all my inhibitions come full swing?

Fightin' 'til there's nothing left of me
Have I given my all?
I persist through my fear
It matters not how big nor how small

All this for the love of the game
Will the game love me the same?
I laboured it all
I still felt Life's squall

Yet it was God
But I laboured more abundantly than them all
Yet not by I
I never seemed to fall to death's call

His grace which was bestowed upon me
Never left me
Thus, as I face what I should fear
I know He is always near

I still have scars from my indiscretions
Anticipating Life's directions
Dodging Life's empty sections
Hurling towards Life's inflections

Yet, He won't steer a parked car
I repent and progress
Can't be the flea in the jar

Looking back on those modest springs
Wondering if I could fly away on one of Cupid's wings
I done seen so much by the time life fold
Now you know why I'm so cold

Peeping around the corner
Wanting to see my destiny
I feel him
My enemy waiting tentatively

They wanna see me smoke on the dough
But I know my demons'll show
I don't wanna die like one of the guys
You see why I wear my disguise?

Ringing loudly
I hear my soul's bells
Tales from the crypt
And all else that ails

These short stories
Nothing less than lessons from my glory
As I part. Remember
Never forget to embrace life's embers.

COMPASSION FOR YOU

ADMIT IT

Hesitating to say love
She strong like
Admit it
You know what's right

You say there's another dude
But you know he don't treat you right
Admit it
Why fight?

Every time you say I'm better
It's runnin' through your head, my pipe
Admit it
What you doin' tonight?

What you see in him is what you see in me?
Look in his eyes, do you see the light?
Admit it
You know you love me with all your might

Dreams of us until I die
Life with you is never trite
Admit it
You see our kids flying kites

Raising kids on your own
It does seem to bite
Admit it
I worry too 'bout the black man's plight

Wonder if I could give you everything & more
To be what you need your black knight
Admit it
You thought 'bout marrying him cuz he White

I'd never thought I say this
My Queens left me in dark of night
Admit it
I'll still achieve but not out of spite

So special cuz you're special
Did you do this out of fright?
Admit it
You took cues from the crew that don't know me, that's who you
cite

I cannot lie
I feel slight
Admit it
You were here, but not quite

Where do we go from here?
Is our future still bright?
Admit it
Do you see our love in the light?

FRENEMY

Fake friends be worse than real enemies.
Lovin you at the top
Then droppin' you on the low?

Call me a friend
Then walk by me like a stranger to no end.

How you blew life into me
Now death into me.
We used to talk so openly
Now you won't look at me.

You're no man
You're no woman
An overgrown child you are
With their cookie in hand.

A friend?
You're no friend to me
I should've known
You'll give your soul
To go where the wind is blown.

Friend to acquaintance
Acquaintance to friend
Why'd I give you a second chance
When I knew how it would end?

Fool me once shame on you.
Fool me twice shame on me.

They warned & told
But I didn't think you'd do that to me.
Be so hurtful & cold.

You used me for what you wanted & what talents you could see
But unbeknownst to thee, I had more up my sleeve.
I was the pad, it felt like you were throwin' darts
There's no other way to describe it
I felt like a tart.

Through 4 I learned to move you from friend to acquaintance
Neverminding whether or not you'll accept my repentance, my
forgiveness.

Crystalizing what I needed to mend
What I Needed in a friend
Through thick and thin.

STAY AWAY

I wish I was sorry
Damn, I wish I was sorry
The love I had for you
That love was never true

Once I knew that was true
I only had 1 thing left to do
But the feeling of you made me cray

Sexin' without affection got old
I'd never thought the south of me would fold
Dreamin' of you was always right
Steady wet from night to night

What I thought was love in the fall
Was actually lust after all
Kissin' on every part
You singing off the chart

With every thrust
Realizing this is a curse
This ain't love
Forever more lust

I didn't know how to stay away
Looks like your heart's left to pay
Don't know how you'll forgive me
Thankful you never left me

Selfish I know
But we both too grown to know
We both played the villain
And the foe

Didn't mean to flip it
But, you too, wanted to hit it

You're two sided
Our vision now divided

You love the Angel and the Demon
You've doubled down live streamin'

What's left next?
Life with you seems like a hex
I'm a mess
Life falling apart; Tetris.

SHOOTER

I see the end before the beginning
I feel like that say it all
You wanna play games?
Don't be mad when I make all dem bodies fall

I breathe
And these fake-o's scoff
Who else you know get kicked out
And still taking off

Better find someone else to play with
I'm not the one bro
You steady laughin'
Don't get tucked like Fredo

Do your best
Don't ever question my hood
Pray to God
Don't let me catch you slippin' in my hood

Do I care?
Hardly
Killin' anyone
Don't mind the bodies

I peepin' that you creepin'
My game sicker than last week's flu
Noticin' you on deep cover
Ridin' with them boys in blue

I'm layin' 'em all down
Only God can stop me
Followin' my beat
Only I can pop me
Made it from southside

All the way to here
Now what makes you think
You is really what I fear

You made a grand mistake
Pushin' your egos
Reading them papers
Gassin' you weirdos

Now you messed up
Should've sniped my head
Now I'm live
You've let loose a thorough bred

I was modest before
Now I want it all
No half steppin'
And Imma have a ball

Just goes to show ya
Come around me you better be prim
Or just do us all a favor
Never wake the one with the dog within.

A MESSAGE TO THOSE WHO ARE UNCLEAR

A message to those who are unclear
What I share here
Isn't out of fear

Just because I love you
Doesn't mean I like you

Take it or leave it
But best believe it
I mean it

Loving all with my heart
Even when others throw darts

So that we're clear
I do love you my dear
But I can't be with you every day in the year

Blood you may be
But that doesn't give you access to me

I value our relationship differently
How can I say this gently?
You chose a different path incidentally

It's not that I don't love you
It's that I don't like you

The choices you've made
Has led to your downgrade
You'll turn my life into a grenade

Strong I know
But life's too short to blow
I need who I'm with to have a vision

I need to achieve my mission
Before life's incision

It's simple
Straight shot
No ripple

When I like you
When I love you
I have unlimited time for you.

COMPASSION FOR OUR COUNTRY

AMERICA'S BLASPHEMY

How you love a negro
But don't support a Negro?
How you IG story a negro
But don't vote for a Negro?

How you taco love a latino
But build a wall 'tween a Latino?
How you vacay in Mexico
And blame it all on the Latino?

The law that's supposed to protect me
Ain't what its purported to be
When I take a kneel
It has nothing to do with those who serve with their will

It's the system that says protect us from them, go kill
But that system won't protect us, they'd rather kill

The flag hurts
Especially when you know
It only works for you in spurts

It pains me so repeatedly
You care so casually
So cavalierly
So nonchalantly

Maybe this time different
Your eyes pinned to the screen
As I vent it

Through every word
I hope you heard
The agony
That lives inside of me
Residing without blasphemy

Your hand on the trigger
Oops
Now lays dead
Just another nigger

I can't take it no more
Too many bodies pilin' on the floor
Covered in fear
Spotlighted like a deer

Scratch that
In this country
I don't deserve an epithet

Black bodies counted
At least the deer gets mounted

Just as the justifications go
My mind lost in the blizzard snow
Realizing you'd rather give to the preservation of wildlife
Rather than the preservation of Black life

Funny how the circle flows
Funny how the circle goes
This is America for better or worse
Sending its colored people to the hearse.

A NOTE TO JOHN

Hear this &
Hear it loud
This is not something new
Someone so proud

Bold in their ways
Yet numbered in their days
I wonder if their power slumbered
In those Arabian days

Ashamed they ought
But valiant they've fought
Some other rather hit that pot
You think he was taught manners as a tot?

There is a pattern
As morally foreign as Saturn
Easy on bad behavior
If you have blonde hair

A soft word turneth away wrath
But, is that the right path?
Unlearning being a follower of the latest trend
Finding comfort on life's eternal bend

The life you live shows on your face
his life is a disgrace
Our home isn't brave
We still have blood from the slaves

It costs you nothing to be kind
Compassion shouldn't have to be mined
Your words are stakes
That makes the world quake

Our leader with no honor
Please be a goner
I beg of you
Bring true peace to your country too.

TYPE

Type privilege, like a White man giving me instructions from his
bmw.
Type life, with rights but don't know how to write.

Type freedom, make me question if I wanna live in the United
Kingdom.
Type shade, where they rather send a brigade than give me a
glass of lemonade.

Type rich, they say we made it, but the rest my people in a ditch.
Type status, make Sherrain turn on Gladys.

Type love, give you a hug after the shove.
Type water, that kills your daughter.

Type immigrant, that's confused at America's
backwards ignorance.
Type country, that promises but never delivers for me.

Type happy, I'm better off without my pappy.
Type thoughts, make me wonder if we'd all understand if we
grew up in Watts.

Type ridicule, positions the question "Did these officials go to
school?"
Type hurt, turn Big Bird & Ernie to curt.

Type vibe, make me pull out my cousin's nine.
Type pattern, they'll never touch the hood rater cover Saturn.

Type heart, makes it hard to turn off its start.
Type missing, the one to be hugging & kissing.

Type poem, force you to question what's real and come
back home.

I WARNED YOU

Bettin' on myself from now
Tired runnin' round with these clowns
My decisions
Of precision

Basic livin' was never my way
Now they ask me to sign the check on payday
Angry at the world
Cast my swine to pearls

Got it backwards
It's going downwards
You didn't think I had it in me
Punched the clock on him pretty quickly

Right to left, left to right
You stuck in a trance
Thought I'd be a simp?
Nah, pay me my advance

Run me what I'm due
You don't wanna see what I can do
Test me, Test me
They must think I'm confetti

Fall from the sky
Every time you try
Nah buddy, this steel
The real deal

Unleashed now
Trynna capture my will
It's too late now
Locked for the kill

Death defying notions
You would've thought I take potions
All my dreams in motion
You would've though Imma natural in the ocean

I go all day, all night
You'll never catch me lackin' on site
This a real scary thing
Now letting heads ring

Told you to let me sleep
Stop botherin' me
Now everything that you loved
I shot up & caught a dub

You learned your lesson?
Never mess with a veteran.
Cuz even when I smile
Know my kill is always on dial.

RIGHTS

It was never 'bout takin' from you
All I want is what I deserve.

Remember…Remember?
Those inalienable rights.

I'm not a killer, but don't push me.
Now I got a race just like me.
And a couple from yours ridin' with me.

1619.
I've been trying to tell you since that time.

But you don't want to listen.
You never listen.
So, now we're here.

I scream defund
And, you run.
I say dismantle it
Then, you gentrify it.
I yell America's lies
Then, you kowtow to 45.

You talk free speech
But, focus on my occupation.
Shut up & dribble.
You tell me be me
While, simultaneously judging me.

Now I've lost that bag
Not only for me
But my family & me
I was better off being a shell of me.

I get the game now
So, I guess the rights for me
Aren't really for me

Exclusively true; they are.
But true for who?

True for you.

4 BLUE

Red handed
Caught like a bandit
Allegories move on
But never tell my story wrong

They grippin' at me
They the prong, I'm the meat
Served in this world
Thought I needed a partner
Thought I needed a girl

Caught with the blood from her heart on my hands again
Thought I could get right
Never thought I lie to the fam

Caught up in the rapture
Runnin' so I don't get captured
Heart beating from time to time
Hoping she'll notice & catch these rhymes

Wanting to love again
Wishing to be 6 & 7 'til 10
Children for life
Holding hands with my wife

Soaking in the rain
Realizing life ain't a game
Realizing the pain in these veins
Don't know if time will change

Crying in pain
Knowing I'll never be the same
Praying life won't be a shame
I wish daddy would've came
Judged by them all

Persecuted to fall
If I go back
They'll ask for a stack

All my cards I dealt
I conquered then left
I've become who I am & that time flew
Strong & gentle
Is my true.

COMPASSION FOR LIFE

DEATH

Journeying through the center of time
Getting to the point until love is sublime

My life I wonder
Will it echo in time?
That is only His choice
The hand of the divine

Did I love faithfully?
Did I love chastely?

I gave my all until the final dung
Each bell that rings
I wonder
If another Angel has sung

Death has its grip on me
I wonder which eternity I'll see

Peace that follows
And, peace that yields
I want to be in heaven
Where Jesus wields

Power and compassion
I wonder if my soul will get any traction?

Envisioning His entrance
Singing with the choirs
Did my heart burn
With Amber fires?

I want to give all I can give
And leave it all on the field

Never the less
Always the more
I never compete with others
I always heal my own sores

Please have mercy on me
I welcome thee

The breaths that come
The breaths that leave
To His breast
I want to cleave

I know now what I must do
To offer my heart up only to you

But wait
Is it too late?
Will the chance to be with you
Soon to dissipate?

I don't know &
I'm not sure
But I've given my all
That's for sure

With peace and tranquility
I learned from you to me

My heart is full
I'm ready to die
That's the truth
There is no lie

With love and ecstasy
I breathe my last breath of death to be.

LIMBS OF THE MAHOGANY

LOVE

I know my private catholic high school experience was not perfect. The institution itself and the people that run it have multiple areas in which they need improvement upon. But, I did see, hear and learn some things of value. One in particular; loving and understanding everyone to the best you can do. No judging. No hating. Learning to be compassionate regardless of the circumstances. This is not exclusive to catholic teachings; it is propagated heavily throughout them. I have a serious internal conflict with those that submit to the Christian faith, went to Christian schools, and/or identify themselves as "good people" when the lack of acknowledgment for the slighting of a group of people's rights, dignity, and opportunity to prosper and be treated equally and fairly have been unrealized. I understand why you might not be fully made aware of these differences (aka injustices) that exist in society. I do not ponder this anymore. But, once you have been made aware of the mistreatment and/or the wrongdoing of one group towards another, I then sit back. I quarrel with the underlying core question of… "well, if my mistreatment, pain, sense of loss, and disenfranchisement has been at least echoed to you (e.g., slavery, police interactions with African Americans that end in African American lives being lost, African American lives being taken away, etc.), what takes precedence to you over that?" Do you not love me too? I ask, "Do you not value my life at all? As you do yours?" These are the questions, as I educate myself, as I reflect, as I view comments and stories and listen to the words from multiple sides of the spectrum (Liberals, Socialists, QAnon, Trump, Conservatives, Evangelical, WASP's, Moderates, etc.) that my mind and heart keep arriving at. Could it be that maybe I believed too heavily in the words and their definitions that can be found in multiple dictionaries such as justice, empathy, compassion, love, community, respect, unity, and harmony, which are etched into the walls and documents of catholic and major religious teachings and instructions? Possibly. Or maybe, just maybe…you need to refocus and reevaluate what you stand for? When you're ready and willing I'm here to talk.

Love,

Josué Casa.

FEAR

Do I make you afraid? Do I intimidate you? When I walk down the street and I see your eyes, I hear your words, I feel your heart. I see your eyes as I lock mine with yours and then yours dart away. I hear your words as you say to a man in a suit and a smile, "You're intimidating". I feel your heart as just the other day when we were alone we poured out our hearts to each other, yet now as we pass each other I am a stranger.

Do I make you afraid? Do I intimidate you? You not realizing that I had to hustle this chocolate charm, this black brilliance, this ebony engenuity, just with the hope and prayer that you would see my personhood. That I, too, make mistakes. That I, too, am not perfect. That I too, while ambitious and confident, want to uplift myself but also you. No games. No ulterior motives. Have you had the courage to ask... "what has he done to make me speak this way, think this way, feel this way about him?" And if that answer, you can voice while staring at yourself in the mirror, is enough evidence for you to validate your words, actions, and feelings, then there is nothing left to say.

TRUTH

Not my "personal truth". Not the opinion that elongates and compacts itself to fit the area of comfort that shifts from situation to situation. No. The truth that is a stake in the ground. The truth that is unequivocal, universal, and self-evident. Yes, the truth may elude us at times. Not because it itself is elusive, but most importantly because we, as humans, have decided to pervert it, distort it, contort it, and ultimately reform it. There is no more blissful ignorance, if there ever was, by coincidence. More than ever, WE have the tools to inform and enlighten ourselves to the history of mankind and the various plights and successes that have been experienced. Yet, you only focus on one media outlet. Yet, you believe what one political party always tells you. Yet, when your source and story is questioned you are immediately defensive. We are so quick to affirm the preconceived notions and biases that ruminate in our minds and hearts. I, too, continue and need to work on this. Now, submit unto you a question, "What does a place look like wherein it's residents do not empathize and sympathize with each other?" Vitriol? Fear mongering? Hate? Misappropriation of truth? Seems to me that we are in that place right now. Don't you? Is this how we want to live? Is this how we want our kids to live?

THE SYSTEM

When did you realize that the system wasn't designed for you?
For me?
Pre-K.

But actually 1st grade.
Maybe that's too raw for you.

How about, when did you realize the system is successful and has
a particular preference for those that have certain qualities?
Can you answer the question?
That's tough because pigs don't know pigs stink.

How do you unplug from the Matrix, when you don't know
you're in the Matrix?
Or you question its validity.
Or you assume everyone has the same moral and value sets as
you
And say, "people wouldn't do that. People wouldn't be pulling the
strings behind some curtain of society that impacts us and you.
Just try harder."
Or you say, "if you get a C, it's because you are lazy and not
trying hard enough."
My friends, that thinking is dangerous.
That thinking is privileged.
While, there are those that are lazy, and that don't try hard
enough, there are those that do that and more and still don't fit
the mold that the system prefers.

Are they not valuable?
Are they not geniuses?
Are they not granted the rewards of success?

Before you make any blanket statement.
Before you conclude your thought process on someone or something.
Look carefully.
Then look critically.

Not just at your own successes and what you persevered through.
But, at the successes of others.

And, hopefully, as I have found you will find that the people that impress, admire and inspire you the most have diverted from the system, sidestepped the Matrix and crafted their own path.

'MERICA

What hope do I have when you can't even say and put actionable
items in place to protect me? Protect those that look like me?
Those that have been negatively affected since this GREAT
country was founded.
Can you say it?
Do you actually believe it's real?
That it has terroristic effects?
That it targets people?

Can you condemn White Supremacy?
Can you say that people of color or quite honestly any person
who does not fit the category of White male has another set of
rules to play by in this GREAT country?
Do you believe any of that to be real?

The White woman jogging at night.
The White man living in impoverished opioid circumstances in
West Virginia.
The Latinx person who fears for their and their parents' life be-
cause at any point ICE can mistake them as illegal.
The black man that makes mistakes in his life, as we all do,
atones for them, only for them to reappear later as a knee is
placed on his neck.
The Muslim person that gets searched 7 times by TSA.
The Jewish person who fears to express their faith and ethnicity
out of fear of retribution.
The black woman who has to make sure everyone else is ok first
before she can be herself.

GREAT country?
My friends, when was 'Merica ever GREAT for everyone?
We can be GREAT.

But we first have to commit to it.
We first must ask ourselves.
Which form of GREAT do we want?
Do we want GREAT just for me and mine?
Or, Do we want GREAT for everyone too?

ACCOUNTABILITY

Sir. Ma'am. Non-binary identifying person. Let me be clear. The presidency does not belong to one person nor one party nor one foreign government. You are its steward. When you take up this mantle of leadership, you revoke certain privileges. You lose the privilege to be sarcastic on the global and national stage about remedies to protecting oneself from a public health crisis. You lose the privilege to brandish remarks about someone or some group's character and aptitude level when they do not agree with you. You lose the privilege to not show human decency, especially in the moments that might take away from the focus being on you. I was taught to respect the office of the president regardless of whom May serve in it. However, how can you respect someone that doesn't respect what and who they serve? You serve me. You are my greatest representative to the world about what it means to be American. And yet, you fail me. And yet, I'm expected to place loyalty, trust and belief in you.

Wow.

LUST

I swore I loved her. I mean, well, I thought I did.
Everything checked out. Her figure, her frame. The intricate
design of the curl of her lips. The way her eyes were almost
a magical wish. Her beautiful hair. The way she and only she
could say my name. Her accent, her voice that soothes me. Her
laugh that I can hear in a crowd of four score. She was deep. We
connected. At least I thought we connected. I asked her to be
mine. And I hers. But all she could see was what she could hear.
She did not want to see me for who I was and for who I am, and
for who I am going to be. She chose the one that was simple to
me. Basic. No flare. No sighted ambition. Nice guy. But it's not
me. I then realized that I am now convincing her to take my
hand as second thought. When if I am all I was, all I am and all
I am going to be, I shouldn't have to beg you to see value in me.
I should be your first string. No more graveling for me. I love Me.
And when she comes along that loves me, I shall love thee. And
we shall love we for all that there is and going to be.

EGO

Gazing into my own reflection. Reading my own press clippings. It barely fulfilled me. Only in vain. Like the midnight snack that kills the hunger at 2 AM. It feels good, your words of uplifting and praise. They do. But are you there when things aren't so cool? When they're more like blue. And your words describe me as a "fool". My ego now confused. I thought you loved me? Or was that all a fluke? Am I not as great as they say or have I truly lost my groove? I used to wear a ring. A championship ring. It was nice. It was shiny. It was big. It captured your attention. I wore it to show you that I had value. That I was somebody. The sad thing is when I didn't wear it, I felt hollow and naked as Adam and Eve did upon their discovery of the knowledge of truth. The truth that my value is not conflated into the ring or into a person or an institution. My value is conflated into God and myself. While your words of encouragement are nice and cool, I do not allow them to overrule. My ego is not how I will die.

GLASS HOUSE

Can you handle it? Yes. Can you handle being looked at for the answers? Yes. Can you handle being the black sheep in rooms? Yes. Can you handle the noise? Yes. Can you handle the betrayal? Yes. Can you handle the false promises? Yes. Can you handle the deceit? Yes. Can you handle being the one they think they know but they really don't? Yes. Can you handle maturing faster than others? Yes. Can you handle hate? Yes. Can you handle overgrown children who call themselves adults? Yes. But would you thrive with all these aspects engaging you at the same time? Yes. Would you be humble throughout it all? I hope. Would you believe that it is only through God, you, and a handful of close people in your life that you are still here right now? Yes. Would you still love those fully who hurt you in ways that they probably don't even realize? I pray. Well then, the choice is yours; it always has been. Will you live in this glass house?

I WANT...

I cannot say if there is that voice inside of you. Your inner you? The "universe"? The Holy Spirit? Whatever you call it, I do not know if that is there like it is there for me. I want people to find that voice and listen to it. I fundamentally believe everyone is born a good person and still has some tie to being a good person. May I appeal to that place that has been avoided in you please? May I have your permission? I want you to feel as I feel. No. I want you to feel as you feel. I want you to place everything in the context of affecting you. What would you feel if you were to be pulled over by a police officer and by the time they knock on your window they already have one hand hovering over their firearm? What would you feel like if you walked out of an elevator and a woman of another race clutched her purse at you while not looking at you in the eye? What would you feel if you found out that people that look like you were being put in detention centers, and dehumanized? Would you feel safe? Would you feel protected? Would you not shake for the uncertainty of your life? Answer that my friend and you might arrive closer to the destination of sentiment that entire races and ethnicities feel. Answer differently my friend, and you might have a more serious problem on your hands than you ought to have contemplated before.

CONTRADICTION

While I know that I am not perfect, I work effortlessly to identify the vices and Achilles' heels that others and myself have. So that, I may learn from them and make the needed adjustments in order to live a better life. Nevertheless, it always befuddles me to see someone exert an exterior force but not remain consistent in exerting the same, if not more, of that same force internally. The contradiction. The hypocrisy. The disconnect is astounding. How can you, as a father, support and give money to the neighborhood, but not to building your own family's dreams? How can you, as a grandmother, love on strangers, but be so negative to your own grandchildren? How can you, as a White student, be a leader in Unified for Uganda, but not frequent the African Student Association or Black Student Association? How can you be involved in an organization similar to a Center for Faith and Justice and not outwardly seek to build relationships with people that are different than you that are right in front of you, occupying space on the very same campus, workplace, and neighborhood you exist in? How can you believe in this part of the Bible or sacred text but not that part? I don't know if these people who behave as such understand the heartbreak, anxiety and impact that their actions cause. Allow me to provide some insight. It feels as if a corner of your heart is falling off. That corner that is being chipped at embodies my faith in people and the institutions they represent. I have to continue to remind myself that it is the individual that is folly not the institution or organization. But I can't do that anymore. That would be naive. There is at times, most times, a larger narrative working that is potentially just as contradictory as the individual who submits to their teachings. And when that is the truth. You can't say the right thing to the wrong person and you can't say the wrong thing to the right person.

GROWTH

From the little black boy who couldn't stop smiling and laughing. To the black boy in an all black school learning about Jesus, his value in the world and in God and the allegiance to his people and country. From the little black boy who won the lottery. To the black boy who now is in a button down plaid shirt and trousers at a diverse school on the other side of town. From the little black boy whose teacher tells him "don't worry about academics just play basketball". To the little black boy who plays chess and scrabble competitively. From the preteen black boy who never played 30 minutes on a school team. To the preteen blackboy who didn't know what to say to girls. From the preteen blackboy who had his first kiss on the dirt path. To the preteen black boy who called the girl he crushed on a bitch. From the preteen boy who got into fist fights and stole from CVS. To the preteen blackboy who got into the selective private catholic high school. From the teen black boy, who wanted to be cool. To the teen black boy that had a chip on his shoulder. From the teen black boy, who didn't have an identity. To the teen black boy, who just wanted to be part of something great. From the teen black boy, who dreamt big. To the teen black boy, who lived abroad. From the teen black boy, who never knew a true friend. To the teen black boy, that graduated with a championship team of brothers. From the young black man, that knew the Midwest would be no easy challenge. To the young black man, who wanted to test himself. From the young black man, that knew not all White people act like this. To the young black man, who questioned where he came from. From the young black man, who was burned at the stake. To the young black man, that learned to love and appreciate his afflicters. From the young black man, who yearned to love his people. To the young black man, that was judged by his people without listening to him.

From the young black man, that learned to love and trust his path. To the young black man, that still walks that walk today.

LOVE FOR ME

THE THREE LOST WORDS

I heard all the words
Except for the ones I deserve
Closed eyes
Lead to desperate cries
All the effort I extended
Yet, still left unattended
My heart still aches
For I never thought she'd flake
Those three words
I love you
Were just for the birds…

Blossoms my heart's fern
Yet, she left me
In Winter's burn

Sharing my heart & soul
Never thought I see
My heart turn coal

Dabbled never in Devil's mold
Shook to my core
I guess love really is fool's gold

I heard all the words
Except for the ones I deserve
Closed eyes
Lead to desperate cries
All the effort I extended
Yet, still left unattended
My heart still aches

For I never thought she'd flake
Those three words
I love you
Were just for the birds…
Say 'em she never could
She knew me all
Yet, not enough good

Dancing on the cliff with my heart
We've come this far
Just to part?

I heard all the words
Except for the ones I deserve
Closed eyes
Lead to desperate cries
All the effort I extended
Yet, still left unattended
My heart still aches
For I never thought she'd flake
Those three words
I love you
Were just for the birds…

Thought I was your love true
It never came
No I love you

I heard all the words
Except for the ones I deserve
Closed eyes
Lead to desperate cries
All the effort I extended

Yet, still left unattended
My heart still aches
For I never thought she'd flake
Those three words
I love you
Were just for the birds...

EBONY

It's not what I know that kills me,
It's what I know for sure that just ain't true.

So then if that's the case &
This is the place, I think.

Think through it all. But for some things, not overthink.

Living here.
Here in this place.
I must face the reality.
Ignorance is not bliss.
Ignorance is death.
Ignorance is death's kiss.

Once you wake up from that blissful sleep,
It makes you wonder
Why didn't they want me to achieve no feat?

It makes me ask,
Did America sell its soul to the Devil?
Was the price cheap?
Just so races with color couldn't be on their level.
Nah, that's too deep.

Can't tell if my mood frustrated or hated.
Cuz everything society says I need
Will never have me saying "I made it!"

Everything they tell me I need
Will never put me on my knees.
Got me prayin' for a way
Cuz they way is a no way
When you look like my type of shay.

Thought once
If I work hard and good
You'd notice my personhood.

But nah.
I had to hustle this Chocolate Charm.
This Caramel Charisma.
This Black Brilliance.
This Ebony Engenuity.

STILL HERE

I'm here.

All ur rumors and lies
Buried me 6 feet deep
With no family ties
Now u wonder why new me seems like a disguise

Ain't this wat u created?
Never had to fake it.
I was over here earnin' dem kites
While you were over there guzzlin' dem natty lites

U say it don't look like I try
Obviously u haven't looked in my eyes
All u would see is the fire
The bread man that just upped to the fries

I'm pushin' the limit
No time for quitin'
Cuz if I do
They'll be no time for winnin'

Only time for mournin'
Heavy dream yearnin'
Over what should've been
But never was turned in

Man in the mirror I'm looking at his reflection
Hopin' I get a deflection
Cuz without one
They'll be no distraction

U wish u were wat u thought u were
I traded money for being popular
While u wanted to be one of them
Funny how I ended up with both of dem

Broken dreams on the street corner
Can't afford to be one of the order
Served up as one of the many on the plate
My moms would look at me and say what a disgrace

Jumped in the game feet first
Now my aspirations lyin' in a hearse
Paid for my actions
These shifty people don't come with no captions

Just wanna get to the finish line
And tell momma I made it
But all they wanna do
Is point at me as the problem
And said we slayed it.

I wasn't designed to fit in
You know what you get from end to end
Don't you remember?
You invited me in.

STRAIGHT UP

Just tell me. Straight up.
Tell me you don't care about me. Tell me I am not worth it. Tell
me you value one race's and ethnicity's life more than mine. Tell
me you want someone else to succeed more than me. Tell me
you could care less about my well-being. Tell me that I shouldn't
strive for my dreams. Tell me that my life in the grand scheme of
things is inconsequential.

Just tell me. Straight up.
Tell me that I will never reach my potential. Tell me that when
I succeed, I make you and others uncomfortable. Tell me I am
just a goofy person. Tell me that I am not smart. Tell me that I
cannot be a master of multiple things. Tell me I am not native
enough to study, at a high level, the foreign language I've spoken
fluently for 7+ years.

Just tell me. Straight up.
Tell me that you trust a less credible individual's opinion on my
reputation and character. Tell me that you are not attracted to
me. Tell me exactly every box you need me to fit into so that you
will accept me. Tell me what I need to do to make you comfort-
able. Tell me that the words that are tattooed across your wall
that you really don't actually want them fully implemented past
the point of your comfort zone.

Just tell me. Straight up.
Tell me that privilege doesn't exist. Tell me your pain is greater
than mine, as if that is really the problem that we are discussing
here. Tell me you are too busy to have a true conversation with
me, but still have the audacity to call me a friend.

Just tell me. Straight up.
Tell me what I create is stupid or incorrect, just because your brain does not comprehend it. Tell me that I am only here because of affirmative action. Tell me that I need to go through the American education system and college and get a masters in order to be successful.

Just tell me. Straight up.
Tell me you really don't have the answers. Tell me you are also figuring it out yourself.

Just tell me. Straight up.
That I and you are not too dissimilar.
That I too dream as you do.
That I too want to be great.
That I too have a heart.

SHADE

Ol' man's river
Turn nigga to darkie
Me speaking old English
Foreign like Farsi

I'm from where the city don't shine bright
For people that ain't that light
Wondering if I should take flight
Or, suffer black man's plight

Thought the answers were in the shade
Lighten it to lighten it
Lighten my shade
Girls'll run down me like a cascade

Mad ill with my tongue
She rather play with a lighter hue 'til kingdom come
We would've had something if you stuck with my hue
Too late, my interest already flew

Thought if I was lighter
My future be brighter
Thought if I was darker
All I'd ever face were the coppers

My shade is beautiful
My shade is whole
I hope, I pray
You don't hollow out my hole.

THE TRUTH I HOLD

The Prince Charming smile. The flirtatious word. The silver
tongue. The fancy clothes. The sharp suit. The loud voice. The
delicious smell.

I guarantee you, you don't know the truth I hold.

The excitement to start. The barriers to break. The records to
shatter. The impressions to make. The business to begin. The
love to lose.

I guarantee you, you don't know the truth I hold.

The lies on me. The envy to me. The toes I stepped. The fear I
felt. The heart I held as it fell out my chest.

I guarantee you, you don't know the truth I hold.

The blizzard drive. The awkward goodbye. The guilt I felt. The
humbling I loathed.

I guarantee you, you don't know the truth I hold.

The tears I cried. The phone with no messages. The mind
that strengthened.

I guarantee you, you don't know the truth I hold.

The refocus I framed. His armor I put on.

I guarantee you, you don't know the truth I hold.

But do you know me?

I guarantee you, you don't know the truth I hold.

THESE PRAYERS

Now I lay myself down to sleep
Even though I've cried
I've never known myself to weep

The friction & the perjury
God can feel the tension & the urgency

My prayer.

Lord protect all those that care
My heart feels them from miles over there

I feel every part personally
Their hurt be hurtin' me

Open me.

Widen me up
So when you're ready
You'll fill me up

They say I'll be a legend soon
Their words I throw to the dunes

Love thee.

By the grace of thee
I am not whole
I am not me & can never be

What I do ask of you
Is something true
To make my heart so full of you.

Amen.

LOVE FOR YOU

HER

To love her
Is to lose her
To not be in search of her

But when I find her
And when I choose her
Will I abuse her?
To love her
But not love her
The way she needs love for her

To love her
Is to lose her
To not be in search of her

For when I close my eyes of her
Appears the silhouette of her
As I wipe the fog of her
Fades the face of her
Left only a memory of her

To love her
Is to lose her
To not be in search of her

I can describe her
The illustrious spirit that's her
The subtle Aurora that's her
Yet she's not mine that's her

To love her
Is to lose her
To not be in search of her

No more will I chase her
Unturned stones are never her
My essence must elude her

To love her
Is to lose her
To not be in search of her

I want to be one with her
To be the team of dreams with her

To love her
Is to lose her
To not be in search of her

Tell me this isn't fantasy.

The fantasy of her.

T.C.

Your very nature perplexes me
You aim to live in luxury
But breathe so callously

Self-styled love's misfit
I offered my love herein for thee
You want love
But silence love's symphony

It all started with a kiss
But you faked any interest
You simply dismissed

Turned to me happily
Said I acted so amiss
I went on my way
Hoping elsewhere I'll find bliss

You went from me to them
No judgement
Even Martin had late night friends

In due time, I'd see you at parties
I loved how you grinded
Pushed up against the wall
The rhythm I had to find it

Still you disappear into the haze
Little did I know
This was a phase

After the house party
My B-day, Senior year
Life is lonely
You call me out of drear

You ask, "Am I wit it?"
Been waitin' for this moment
You know I'm wit it

My mindset
Straight to the point, no zag
Came prepared
2 doms & a sleeping bag

After all this dirty talkin' it
You say, "After thinkin' it
I'm not feelin' it"
I'm mad steamin' it

Relaxin' & Relatin'
I ask her
"This whole time you playin?"

She retort back
"No just not in the mood"
I sit back thinking
"Man, I could've ate some good food"

We wake up & yawning
She rollover & say
"It's time for you to go darling"

Now that was the last try
I'm cool on your vibe
I don't like games
And. Yours I definitely don't subscribe

My, my how time flies
5 months go by
Now you want to try

You want to date me?
I laugh because it's funny
Darling, that ship has sailed
You must think I'm a dummy

Move in with you?
Your brain, you dropped
In a pile of doo-doo

Ridiculous
Funny you are & funny you stay
You can't always have it when you want it
Ms. Sharpay

Yet & still you move out here
Common sense left astray
Close to my people's house
6 minutes away

With no money, no job in fact
You get lonely
And, buy a cat?

Can't forget

You felt sorry
Now you sign their lease
Your sister's & her mari

Finances set up for a deathwish
How are you not reddish?
With you, I'd perish

Glad you said no
Glad I did too
For being with you never flow
Cuz me as me would never grow.

IN SPITE

Blessed & highly favoured
The love I had for you never waivered
From country to country
I always have the munchies

No doubt I crave you
You're my appetite through & through
I shake, I shiver
Without you? My soul quivers

Did you hear that rhyme?
With that simple finishin' line
My love doth grow
When right what we sow

Elegance beyond our years
We do laps 'round our peers
No gamble on life at all
I sneak 7's off the corner wall

Candlelight burning love's flame
Losing it all, will she love me the same?
How can I tell her the fall?
I lost it all

Rainy day upon us
This year we might miss Christmas
The love I had for you was never old
The love I have for you is still bold.

LOVE AGAIN — ODE TO MAYA

A kiss, a hug, a brush
Her touch was effortless
To know what love is
And lose it in a rush
Will there ever be a chance for me to depend?
On that love I've seem to lost again
With all my might
With all my soul
I pray to God to lend
Just once more
That simple love again

Roses are red
Violets are blue
That's so old
You can finish that too

Not impressed by the rest
All I want is you
To hold in my hands
To know what we share is true

The surprises I discover
Finding myself in the serendipitous of you
Are you my kin?
Kin of soul? Now that is true

A kiss, a hug, a brush
Her touch was effortless
To know what love is
And lose it in a rush
Will there ever be a chance for me to depend?
On that love I've seem to lost again
With all my might
With all my soul
I pray to God to lend
Just once more
That simple love again

I wonder if you know what I know
Only way to heal is to trust
Nevertheless, you must confess
Or our love will evaporate, simply combust

What is it that you want?
The courage to love
Well darling, darling, darling
That doesn't come without a shove

A kiss, a hug, a brush
Her touch was effortless
To know what love is
And lose it in a rush
Will there ever be a chance for me to depend?
On that love I've seem to lost again
With all my might
With all my soul
I pray to God to lend
Just once more
That simple love again

While these are the facts of life
Some men come for sex & whatever else is in store
While others
Some men come to heal & restore

A kiss, a hug, a brush
Her touch was effortless
To know what love is
And lose it in a rush
Will there ever be a chance for me to depend?
On that love I've seem to lost again
With all my might
With all my soul
I pray to God to lend
Just once more
That simple love again.

RAP

Aye yo ma
Lemme flirtate
Let me holla at you
Let a visionary vibrate

I know you know this
But, you summertime fine
Off the into, I might just marry you
You wedding time fine

Nah, matter fact
You winter time fine
Made from Him
My love for you is so divine

First q, counting my pockets
All the money in the world
Wanna hit you in that spot you love
Make your toes curl

Got a brutha wonderin tho
Is it better to be poor & love?
Or should I do what they do?
Be rich with no dove

When you smile
Lighting flash across my body
My moms was wrong
You ain't just no hottie tottie

Thinking out loud
Rhyming to rhyme's end
I can't be another guy
Counting the seconds 'til I'm past best friend.

MY EVERYDAY LOVE STORY

Go head lemme see it.
You trynna let me feel it.
I wanna be in it.
Don't play no tricks wit it.

You gonna lemme feed it.
She told me lemme eat it.

Please it,
bring it,
meet it.
Am I still urs if I free it?

I wanna be it.
Do you need it?
We be freakin' it,
While I be one kneein' it.
Now we be in the room heavy breathin' it.

Eye to eye, we glarin' it.
Legs shakin' wit it.
Can't believe it.
Look what we done in it.

Heart to hear, beat matchin' it.
Thinkin' I might plan B it.
Cold sweatin' it.
Do I leave it?

Manhood checkin' it.
Better or worse when I said it, I meant it.

Let her know I ok it.

Hand holdin', 9 monthin' it.
Water breakin' it.
Heart beatin', sweaty palmin' it.

Palm grippin', heavy breathin' it.
She steady pushin' it.
Doc grim facin' it.

No pulse checkin' it.
We knew it.
We lost it.

Cryin' through it.
Askin' God how could he do it.

Prayin' for an answer to it.
Leanin' on you.
Leanin' on Him.
Leanin' on us.
To get me through.

HAVE

How can you have a wife & not love her?
Treat her right?
Make sure she has everything she needs
Before you go to sleep at night.

How can you say you love her?
When you meeting her needs
Is second to others...

How can you call yourself a man when her back aches?
& all you want to do is watch basketball tapes?

What happened to the vows?
What happened to the promises?
Now I'm a doubtful Thomas.
Wondering if real love is real or is it all just fake.

Yet and still I see examples of what it takes to be a good mate.
To die to yourself and behold her eternal beauty.
That's why I wear black and she wears White.

I am a man.
Not a male with a zipper.

I want you.
I need you.
As I prepare for you.

I learn
So, I know how to be &
How not to be
When I'm with you.

For, as the wise man once said to the foolhardy man who asked,
"When should I tell my wife I love her?", he replied back to him
"Before someone else does".

I mean what I say &
Say what I mean.
I will always say to you
You are my dream.
I love you.

M.B.C.

When she knows my heart.
Even when it's bitter & tart.
When she holds me accountable,
Even when I'm not able.

When she knows my spirit's song
Sometimes playing it too long.

When she'll have me triple guessing the right move,
Then tell me just to make the move.

When she lives with no regret in the moment,
Even when I'm scared if I passionately act she'll lament.

When she is my peace, and I'm her's.
When she can be she &
I can be me.

When it's obvious we belong together,
Yet & still she's hard to tether.

When her dreams are mine &
We want them at the same time.

Where she struggles,
I prosper.
Where I fall,
She soars.

MBC to MBL.

More Black Love.

S.G.D.

When I first saw you, words became old.
If young me met present me
He would've said love at first rip was a no go.

I believe, I believe. But do I?
Is this what I think it is?
Love at first sight.

All cool leaves me.
Now she sees me.

But I know that I know.
But you don't see me as I see you.
That I want to be everything you want.
That I want to be everything you need.

It's more than the physical.
It's your mental.
It's your spiritual.

All these other guys that just wanna get in your fly.
I won't ever be, I'll never try.

I want to be your everything.
Something that every woman needs.

As I look back around.
I fumbled on a couple downs.

Me being too chary
Left dead our intimacy.

When you put your heart in my hand,
I felt first I needed to be a friend.
A friend like your parents.
One that you can love.
You can trust.
That will always try & never fuss.

Maybe my mind moved too fast,
Thinking of your first next to my last.
Kneeling by our bed.
Changing the world hand in hand.

Spent my whole life prayin' for someone like you,
All to find out, you don't feel to me as I to you.
Playin' love songs 'til I dream,
Now I know what they really mean.

No more I know what's fun,
All I think of is Tennyson
Was he true at all?
'Tis better to have loved & lost
Than never loved at all.

To feel my heart bust
Cuz I know all before was lust.
Tried & true these are the pieces of love,
That float away like His dove.

Finding parts of it within my own creases,
Shattered on the floor my heart's pieces.

In my life, I still cherish
For without you I shall perish.

Memories they will be
Bout what could be.
What should be.
What would be.
What will be.
If only thee, would let it be.

With open arms & all of me,
I hope you find it with or without me.
With faith,
Love JH.

ARRIVE

Will she arrive like a present at my front door?
Or will we meet in the middle of the moonlit dance floor?
Will her smile glisten through her face mask?
Or will she be another stranger that I walk past?

Either way it's weighing on me.
I close my eyes knowing I'll see her in my dreams.
What do I say to her?
Do I tell her that she is everything that is me
and everything I want to be?

Is that too forward or too basic?
I dream she'll stay.
But truth is she just might run away.

The more I talk with her the more I realize
Life without her will be just fine.
Ur life with her will be solely divine.
I'll change her life as she changes mine.

But will she accept me as I accept her?
In all my ways that hurt.
In all my ways that need work.

I hope,
I pray,
That she will see me as I see her.
As the one for me
That will push me
To be all that I can be.

As the one for her
That will push her
To be all that she can be.

I hope,
I pray,
That she will see me
As one that deserves thee.
To say and mean unequivocally,
"I love you.
You are my life.
And, it is a privilege to be by your side
through success and strife".

WITHOUT YOU

You're second to none. Without you, there is no fun.

Win the game, get the award, feed the fame
Without you, it'll never be the same.

Singing Babyface, Luther, & Curtis
Without you, they just don't flourish.

Oh captain! My captain!
Like the captain who dies,
As her reaches his prize
Without you, my heart's the same,
Pullin into shore in vain.

If I ever get to heaven,
I'll make sure I'll tell the reverend,
Without you it's not the 7.

While I know who I am &
Whose I am,
Without you I'm damned.

Mind runnin', maybe if I'll achieve
Feelings will leave,
But,
Without you, plans are dead like King Tut.

When you needed me I was there,
Without you, I seem not to care.

Without you I do feel sad &
Alone cuz,
Without you, there just ain't
No buzz.

As time closes I wonder,
Without you, will life have its thunder?

Through reflection I've found what I'm prone,
Without you, I've grown.

All the opportunities I've blown,
I still hear you moan.

It's time for something new,
Without you, is cool.
I've learned to be patient for what's in love's folds,
Without you, is part of love's road.

VOYEUR

She previews and peruse
But never seems to infuse.
I want to recuse but
She might bemuse and confuse
Then accuse. Thus, I must
Amuse to diffuse. Yet and still,
I want to enthuse
Rather than misuse.
I need to transfuse and perfuse
But she just might, just might refuse.

Those that can't read between lines.
I'll make it plain just one time.

She previews and peruses my poems,
But never seems to infuse herself as character in them
I want to recuse her about her actions,
But she might bemuse and confuse them in factions.
Then accuse me
And without a word flee.
Thus, I must amuse her with my charm,
To diffuse her from any harm.
Yet and still, I want to enthuse her presence,
Rather than misuse her essence.
I need to transfuse and perfuse how I feel about her,
But she just might, just might, refuse my fleur.

LOVE FOR OUR COUNTRY

AMERICA'S STORY

America oh America
Shouldn't I have known
Your fair weathered ways
Nothing more than a bust

America oh America
How you've ladened me
How I believed you
So effortlessly

America oh America
I do believe in your good deeds
But why do they come
So distant and rarely consistently

America oh America
To fight for you
To fight for a state
That doesn't see my color as true

Know His Story.
Say his name
Or will they simply fade away
Into the depths of vain?

Know Her Story.
Say her name
Or will they simply fade away
Into the depths of vain?

Know Their Story.
Say their name
Or will they simply fade away
Into the depths of vain?

I can't help but think...Am I next though?
Will I be another metric?
As their prisons' hoe

Blindfold on or off
It's a decision
It's a choice
Not to scoff

Well I'm here now
What more could you possibly want from me?
I have given it all
My affinity

America oh America
Shouldn't I have known
Your fair weathered ways
Nothing more than a bust

America oh America
How you've ladened me
How I believed you
So effortlessly

America oh America
I do believe in your good deeds
But why do they come
So distant and rarely consistently

America oh America
To fight for you
To fight for a state
That doesn't see my color as true

Know His Story.
Say his name
Or will they simply fade away
Into the depths of vain?

Know Her Story.
Say her name
Or will they simply fade away
Into the depths of vain?

Know Their Story.
Say their name
Or will they simply fade away
Into the depths of vain?

I've given you my all
I've given you my soul
And now we stand here
And we've watched it all fall

I must wonder
Will our better angels persevere?
I must ponder
Will the average man be a believer?

America oh America
Shouldn't I have known
Your fair weathered ways
Nothing more than a bust

America oh America
How you've ladened me
How I believed you
So effortlessly

America oh America
I do believe in your good deeds
But why do they come
So distant and rarely consistently

America oh America
To fight for you
To fight for a state
That doesn't see my color as true

Know His Story.
Say his name
Or will they simply fade away
Into the depths of vain?

Know Her Story.
Say her name
Or will they simply fade away
Into the depths of vain?

Know Their Story.
Say their name
Or will they simply fade away
Into the depths of vain?

My color should not be what puts me in death's way
I need you to understand this so intrinsically
You can never admit the truth
Your morals move so capriciously

America oh America
Shouldn't I have known
Your fair weathered ways
Nothing more than a bust

America oh America
How you've ladened me
How I believed you
So effortlessly

America oh America
I do believe in your good deeds
But why do they come
So distant and rarely consistently

America oh America
To fight for you
To fight for a state
That doesn't see my color as true

Know His Story.
Say his name
Or will they simply fade away
Into the depths of vain?

Know Her Story.
Say her name
Or will they simply fade away
Into the depths of vain?

Know Their Story.
Say their name
Or will they simply fade away
Into the depths of vain?

TYPE

Type privilege, like a White man giving me instructions from his
bmw.
Type life, with rights but don't know how to write.

Type freedom, make me question if I wanna live in the United
Kingdom.
Type shade, where they rather send a brigade than give me a
glass of lemonade.
Type rich, they say we made it, but the rest my people in a ditch.
Type status, make Sherrain turn on Gladys.

Type love, give you a hug after the shove.
Type water, that kills your daughter.

Type immigrant, that's confused at America's backwards ignorance.
Type country, that promises but never delivers for me.

Type happy, I'm better off without my pappy.
Type thoughts, make me wonder if we'd all understand if we
grew up in Watts.

Type ridicule, positions the question "Did these officials go to
school?"
Type hurt, turn Big Bird & Ernie to curt.

Type vibe, make me pull out my cousin's nine.
Type pattern, they'll never touch the hood rater cover Saturn.

Type heart, makes it hard to turn off its start.
Type missing, the one to be hugging & kissing.

Type poem, force you to question what's real and come back home.

UNITY

Does your unity increase the peace?

Unity that inspires.
Unity that uplifts.
Unity that seeks to mitigate disenfranchisement.

Unity that creates equity & fairness for all.
Unity that loves.
Unity that embraces.
Unity that is compassionate.
Unity that is humble.

Unity that seeks to listen first rather than speak.
Unity that extends an olive branch before a weapon.
Unity that loves openly & fully rather than hate internally
& boldly.

Unity that says you first & shows it by demonstrating it.
Unity that disagrees, but respects.
And, unity that learns & matures.

LOVE FOR LIFE

THE COLORS OF LIFE

Here's the thing, and there's really no way of gettin' round it.

Loving to the maximum is how you're supposed to live it.

Time never seems to fly for me,
I pack so much into every moment of me.
1 year seems like 3.

Work hard, play hard is the mantra
But to my generation, it seems like that's old fashioned
Like prima nocta.

To achieve is to breathe
It's a habit to me
As others look upon thee
While they thumb teethe

Hands in pockets
Blazin' like rockets
Not a goal in sight
They wonder why I'm in flight.

Now they're blue
I tell 'em it's not just for me
It's for you too.

Now they're green
Plottin' on a way to scheme
As I sidestep
They fret.

Now they're red
Searchin' for a way to make me dead
"Friends" on in the action
My enemies I've yet to mention.
I just wanna stay gold
Like Robbie Frost once told
Society won't let it happen
Ignorance is bliss captain.

Silver tongued
Life's supposed to come easy to no end
But reality sinks in
I am just a man.

I look in the mirror to find I'm brown
Makes me wonder if that's the reason this all goes down
America's relentless efforts to make me drown.

Some of us believed the orange one
Now we're more divided just for fun
He's a reflection of us
Now how do we save us from us?

Livin' between the margins, black and White
Until I die it's going to be a fight
Energy expended
With those that swear they defend it.

Freedom is found in the gray area
Like a right pro-lifer at a Black Lives Matter feria
Until we accept fact as fact
We'll never get past that's what that's.

Here's the thing, and there's really no way of gettin' round it.

Each day u wake it's one more step closer to death, but if u make each step full of life, when the time comes, you will never be one of those cold, regretful and fearful people that never knew love at its maximum nor success at its fullest pearl.

TO GIVE EVERYTHING

I got too many gifts
You ain't play fair
You gonna set a bad example for the average bear

What they said
They told me these lies
I used to believe 'em to great surprise

Their whole base was envy
I had to refocus
Had to prove my success wasn't hocus pocus

Helping those that want to be helped
Humbled myself past fear
No longer did I need their cheer

Clear as ever
Imma show 'em how to make it here
Show 'em how to make it there

Knew if they killed me
Knew if they took it there
I ain't gonna care

Almost done
Achieved my mission
In spite their disposition

As I reflect
All my story
Filled with glory

No regrets ever left
I laid it all on the field
With that I can deal.

THE TRUTH OF ME

Mind racing
My thoughts in entropy
Got me nervous
Don't know if I'll ever find the theme in me

Only one try in this life stance
Wonder if I'll get a partner to enjoy the dance

Walking the road
Smelling the flowers
At every turn
Life towers

Life's challenges appear at the fork
Striving to push my dreams past the cork

No dreams
No power
Swear I'll never be 'em
One of those cowards

Living life's journey
I feel the burn of the tourney

Smelt the rose
Distant red horns
Got too close
Now I have thorns

Life's waters I want to swim in
Too bad you a dim kin

Thorns on me everywhere
Now I'm the tortoise, not the hare
As if anyone cared
My securities locked in the lair

Life forcing me to choose who gonna stay
Life force me to choose who have to stay away

I'm only one man
I have to accept that plan
What's next
Surely will vex

Life got me trusting in God a lot
He can't steer a car stuck in the lot

Focused on achieving 'til the end
All I come to in my thoughts
I give what I give
And, give it all I've got

Life's endless mysteries
Simply straight clear to me

Here's what I know
As I ruffle through this trove
I don't want to be empty & cold
Never to be fulfilled & bold

Life's pleasures come in abundance
Life's pains come in redundance

The day you're born into this menace
Is really a death sentence
The day you're born into this gift
You gotta make it right swift

Life will yield what you give
Life is about leaving it all on the field

Overcome my fears
Destined for cheers
No longer do we give patronage to the likes of those
The Lears

You will never define my life
I am my own light

The truth is truth no matter what feat
Some use tools to kill, others to treat
Realizing the truth in this beat
That I'm only better than the person I used to be.

LET'S BE CLEAR

Mahogany: Reflections of a Young Black Man is a collection of poetry focused on the telling of an individual who does not solely fit the stereotypical, limited, and mundane archetypes that society has to offer at this point. This individual is me. This individual is you. This individual is us. How do you love someone when they don't love you back? How do you love a system that doesn't protect you? How do you love a country that fears you? The reflections I have to offer you are those of a 22-year-old; who urges us all to just be a little more compassionate. Hopefully through these poetic ensembles you too may be just a little more compassionate to your fellow person.

AUTHOR BIO

Josué Casa is a poet, thought-leader, and strategic consultant that prides himself on tackling the nuanced challenges society inadvertently and intentionally finds itself in. He strives to uplift all people that are committed to the progression of society that is equally beneficial for everyone. Josué, being one who matured in 4 countries before the age of 23, realizes the beauties and serendipities that are in conjunction with American, but he consistently challenges the notion that we--as a society--have arrived. That we as a race...the human race are at the point of true and full compassion for our fellow person. Josué's greatest mentor once told him, "Always keep revisiting your dreams". In everything Josué partakes in, it aligns with maintaining compassion and love and wanting the best for everyone.

Made in the USA
Monee, IL
10 May 2022

96145130R10079